Execution and Other Lessons

Notes on Entrepreneurial Thought Leaders Volume 3 (2007-2008)

PersonalOpz

This book is for sale at
http://leanpub.com/execution_and_other_lessons

This version was published on 2014-02-10

This is a Leanpub book. Leanpub empowers authors and publishers with the Lean Publishing process. Lean Publishing is the act of publishing an in-progress ebook using lightweight tools and many iterations to get reader feedback, pivot until you have the right book and build traction once you do.

This work is licensed under a Creative Commons Attribution-ShareAlike 3.0 Unported License

Tweet This Book!

Please help PersonalOpz by spreading the word about this book on Twitter!

The suggested hashtag for this book is #execution.

Find out what other people are saying about the book by clicking on this link to search for this hashtag on Twitter:

https://twitter.com/search?q=#execution

Also By PersonalOpz

Passions and Other Lessons

Capital is No Longer a Constraint

Cut the Lifeboats

Start Making Dreams

Ideas Are a Dime a Dozen

Thanks to Stanford University for this inspiring resource. And my family for further inspiration and support. And to Andrea–beat the big C!

Contents

Preface 1

From Venture Capitalist to Entrepreneur 3

Lessons from the Electric Roadster 5

Startups: The Need for Speed 6

The Art of Negotiation 8

The Growth of Solar Ventures 11

Connecting Common Experiences 12

Delivering a Digital Torrent 15

How to Build a Successful Company 16

Angel Investing Revealed 18

Intersection of the Environment and Financial Markets 21

CONTENTS

- Entrepreneurial Practices for High-Impact Non-Profits 23
- The Path to an Acquisition 24
- Healthy Entrepreneurship in Medical Devices 26
- Representing the Socially Responsible Enterprise 28
- Banking on Corporate Culture and Strategy 30
- Entrepreneurship That Clicks 32
- Concentrated Power in a Global Economy 34
- Rewarding Sky-High Innovation 36
- Unreeling the Documentary Film 38
- The Evolution of Yahoo! 39
- The Next Wave of Corporate Philanthropy 40
- Under the Microscope: Socially Responsible Biotech 41
- A VC Perspective on the Life Sciences 43
- Music Artists Go Entrepreneurial 44
- Thanks for Reading 46

Preface

A pretty consistent theme in my third volume of notes on the Entrepreneurial Thought Leaders series was doing big things:

"Go big or don't go." - Donna Novitsky (Big Tent)

"Go big." - Brett Crosby (Google Analytics)

"Go for broke and fail big." - Anand Chandrasekaran, Michealene C. Risley (Tapestries of Hope)

If you're going to dedicate years of your life doing something then it does make sense to make that something meaningful and to spread it as wide as possible. The Internet has enabled companies, charities, and individuals to scale their efforts like never before. Social networking has given everybody the ability to get their message heard both near and far. Businesses are now leveraging talent around the world to build products used around the world. In short, it is easier than ever to go big.

However I feel that message, by itself, discounts the efforts of millions of entrepreneurs who are creating businesses for their local communities or smaller niches. Even those with global aspirations have to start somewhere. In fact starting small and building the minimum viable product is one of the foundations of the lean startup movement.

"To the world you are one person but to one person you are the world." - Card my wife gave me

Entrepreneurs come in all shapes and sizes. I salute all of you.

Will

From Venture Capitalist to Entrepreneur

Date: 2007-10-03

Speaker: Donna Novitsky (Big Tent)

Link: Entrepreneurial Thought Leaders[1]

When seeking first funding think about what is the next inflection point where I remove risk from this venture?

Align milestones with rounds of funding.

There are only 24 hours in a day.

Go big or don't go.

The best V.C.s are former entrepreneurs and operating executives.

V.C.s work primarily at a strategic level.

The entrepreneur's job is execution.

Build the best team you can possibly build.

You can't do it alone.

Incredibly bright people can fail because they are afraid to delegate.

---

[1] http://ecorner.stanford.edu/authorMaterialInfo.html?mid=1815

Balance takes place over a long period of time.

Learn to juggle.

You have to be able to spell a company name. You have to be able to get the URL. It is helpful if it is memorable.

People find all ways to contribute far beyond their job description.

Wall Street asks different questions than customers ask.

Cash is king in a startup.

Spend the company's money like you spend your own.

Before you can market you need to have marketing strategy.

Lessons from the Electric Roadster

Date: 2007-10-10

Speaker: Martin Eberhard (Tesla Motors)

Link: Entrepreneurial Thought Leaders[2]

Work on something you care about.

Electric cars push the choice of fuel upstream.

One key to being a successful entrepreneur is naivety. If you know how hard a problem is when you set out you won't do it.

Big idea was to use lithium ion batteries because of the density.

Face reality.

You need to balance a team with a combination of smarts, experience, passion and enthusiasm.

Products start at high end of market but as supply chain matures the price goes down.

---

[2] http://ecorner.stanford.edu/authorMaterialInfo.html?mid=1816

Startups: The Need for Speed

Date: 2007-10-17

Speaker: Dominic Orr (Aruba Networks)

Link: Entrepreneurial Thought Leaders[3]

The productivity of your employees can be maximized by giving each one of them freedom and trust.

Every product you build has to fit into the ecosystem of the big guys but solves a problem they cannot fix.

It all boils down to speed. Speed of innovation. Speed of execution.

Big companies have to stay the course.

It is not just speed but thoughtful speed.

If you want to go for thoughtful speed then you have to trade off with a lot of discussion and analysis versus going with your gut.

Don't defend with your ego. Let intellectual honesty dictate.

For people to be thick-skinned they have to be confident.

---

[3]http://ecorner.stanford.edu/authorMaterialInfo.html?mid=1817

Not everybody is as comfortable with themselves as you think they are.

IPO process is more about branding than bringing cash.

The Art of Negotiation

Date: 2007-10-31

Speaker: Stan Christensen (Arbor Advisors)

Link: Entrepreneurial Thought Leaders[4]

Conventional wisdom about negotiation is often wrong.

Almost all negotiations in life repeat (you see the person more often than once) yet most people negotiate as if it is a one time deal.

Natural talent helps with negotiation but education helps a lot.

There is hope for everyone in being effective at negotiation.

Tactics shouldn't be your primary method of negotiating.

Figure out how to expand the pie as opposed to just dividing up the pie.

Be open to questioning your assumptions.

People that spend time together have a hard time not questioning their assumptions.

Fundamentally negotiation is about how to have relationships and manage them effectively.

---

[4]http://ecorner.stanford.edu/authorMaterialInfo.html?mid=1819

Criteria are objective standards that are independent of what either side wants.

Precedent is always a criteria you can use.

It is important to base your agreement on things that are objective not just what one party wants or another party wants.

Listening isn't just a nice thing to do. It can be extremely persuasive in negotiations.

People often have more in common than they think.

Agreements are worked out within the context of relationships.

If you're good at relationships you're good at negotiation.

There is no objective measure of success in the War on Terror.

Most people don't systematically prepare for negotiations which is a big mistake. There is a direct correlation between how much somebody prepares and how well they do in negotiations.

Never lie and there are no exceptions.

Can you get stuff done? If you're trustworthy it is easier to get stuff done.

Apologize more. It doesn't cost you anything.

It is much easier to find out what you can do and what you can change than what they can do better and they can change.

Stay in the game.

Give them extra. There are always opportunities in negotiations to make it a little bit better for the other side. People are surprised and reciprocate.

You can make it better for them without making it worse for you.

If somebody is going to lie to you then the last thing you want to do is attribute something to them.

Always have a BATNA (Best Alternative to a Negotiated Agreement) going in.

There are a lot of gender differences in how people approach negotiation.

Look at issues as a package rather than going issue by issue. Look at negotiations as packages of issues.

The Growth of Solar Ventures

Date: 2007-11-07

Speaker: Larry Bawden (Jadoo Power)

Link: Entrepreneurial Thought Leaders[5]

With change there is opportunity.

Everybody should check out and do a sabbatical at least twice.

You learn a lot of things in startups by hindsight.

People are genuinely concerned about global problems (climate change, oil prices, population, resources).

Global problems drive change in governments.

You want to get something that works. You want to scale it. You want to start building revenues.

Integrated storage solution is what is missing for solar.

---

[5]http://ecorner.stanford.edu/authorMaterialInfo.html?mid=1820

Connecting Common Experiences

Date: 2007-11-07

Speaker: Armen Berjikly, Julio Vasconcellos (Experience Project)

Link: Entrepreneurial Thought Leaders[6]

Experience Project brings people together around their shared life experiences to build support groups, etc.

Anonymity is a key to the site.

When you're starting a social site on the Internet you want to echo what cavemen have been doing since fire (rather than building something new).

Multiple sclerosis tends to strike young women in their early 20s. Inflammations in the brain can lead to paralysis, cognitive issues, or nothing.

People who post on health sites are not doing well. Survivors are either out doing things or don't want to show how well they're doing.

When you start a company you're going to violently close almost all of the doors in your life as you pursue one of them.

---

[6]http://ecorner.stanford.edu/authorMaterialInfo.html?mid=1821

It takes much longer than you think.

Silicon Valley seems like a huge place but it really is about 150 people who have influence.

You constantly need to overcome the credibility gap.

If people see advertising that is relevant to them it is okay.

You need to work with people who have been there and done that.

Mentor capitalist is somebody who has faced the same struggles.

You need someone who can say it is alright. Zoom out for a second.

You need people who can guide you.

You really don't know what you don't know.

The culture of the site is set at the very beginning.

Hiring is hugely important for a startup. You spend more time with them than anything else.

Investors are good at helping you find VPs and CFOs but they're not good at helping you find developers.

It is so hard to find good developers that it is okay to go through a recruiter.

If you don't have passion for your project you're going to get exhausted, spin your wheels, and eventually give up.

Every single day people are going to be questioning what you're going to do.

Spend what you raise.

You're part of a very large flow. Relationships exist beyond you and after you.

You can not underestimate the value of having some experience in the corporate world.

Unless you have a patentable idea stealth doesn't work.

In the end it is execution.

When you have no money to pay someone you use your equity. What it is worth is a long discussion.

As an entrepreneur you will probably underestimate what you need to raise. Your angels will help you push that number up.

Delivering a Digital Torrent

Date: 2007-11-28

Speaker: Ashwin Navin, Ping Li (BitTorrent)

Link: Entrepreneurial Thought Leaders[7]

Linux distributions were the first to really start using BitTorrent.

BitTorrent is fundamentally a delivery protocol and the company is fundamentally a delivery service.

People increasingly want to consume entertainment online, on their PCs, or on their connected devices.

There is no sustainable business model in criminalizing customers.

There isn't just one open source license.

Open source is not a model for every business.

Open source is good for developing a community of developers early on.

The real value of open source is distribution. You get free distribution.

---
[7]http://ecorner.stanford.edu/authorMaterialInfo.html?mid=1822

How to Build a Successful Company

Date: 2008-01-16

Speaker: Mitch Kapor (Foxmarks)

Link: Entrepreneurial Thought Leaders[8]

Interest in the wisdom of crowds.

Competing with big giants is a bad idea and should be avoided.

The barriers to entry of startups are enormously lower than they were a generation ago.

If you're going to build a business that has value you're going to need to solve somebody's problem.

Raising money creates accountability.

Picking an investor is like picking a cofounder.

It is all about the people.

You have to execute.

Have corporate values and measure performance on them.

---

[8]http://ecorner.stanford.edu/authorMaterialInfo.html?mid=1901

You can't layer social responsibility onto a business like icing on a cake.

Business that are ahead of the curve on sustainability will do better on average. (Warren Buffett meets the Sierra Club)

There will be opportunities to do great businesses based on doing the right thing.

Unleash people to do what they couldn't do before.

Angel Investing Revealed

Date: 2008-01-23

Speaker: Ron Conway, Mike Maples Jr. (Angel Investors)

Link: Entrepreneurial Thought Leaders[9]

An angel investor is somebody who invests $50k or $100k in raw startups.

The angel investor term was started in the 30s as somebody who invested in movies in LA.

The good angels have had some type of accomplishment in business before.

Good angels will provider a broader range of exit options.

Ideas are pretty cheap.

The average angel round is $500,000 to $1,000,000.

Avoid codependencies.

It is not the entrepreneur that failed. It is the business that failed. In life you win some and you lose some.

Fail gracefully.

---

[9]http://ecorner.stanford.edu/authorMaterialInfo.html?mid=1902

The entrepreneurs that fail are the ones that didn't understand that the business was supposed to morph.

Companies that have low burn rates have hugely larger probabilities of getting lucky over time.

Companies are the most productive when they are less than ten people.

Have a customer development strategy in addition to a product development strategy.

Don't scale until it works.

Discover the business–don't scale the business.

Too much money in a startup is toxic. It causes you to pursue losing strategies for too long to the detriment of the winning strategies.

Silicon Valley isn't so much of a place as an idea about what is possible and what kind of companies can be built. People that gravitate towards that set of ideas and culture gravitate there.

In the hyper competitive world of startups every advantage counts.

Exit isn't a number but a probability distribution curve.

Who you choose to trust is one of the most important things to do in your entrepreneurial career.

If an idea is truly disruptive it is always capital efficient.

Capital efficiency is a religion for how you can run a business.

You don't start a company yourself–you need to go and collaborate with people.

You have no excuse in life not to do things you're passionate about.

If you're doing something you're not passionate about you're flunking a cosmic I.Q. test.

Most decisions are 50/50 or obvious.

You need to give yourself permission to do the thing you know is the right thing.

Commit yourself to doing exceptional work always.

Intersection of the Environment and Financial Markets

Date: 2008-01-30

Speaker: Jesse Fink, Steve Blank (Priceline, Serial Entrepreneur)

Link: Entrepreneurial Thought Leaders[10]

The issues are so large with climate change that technology will enable the solutions but there are business model issues and systematic issues that need to be addressed.

The issues in clean energy are innovation and commercialization.

Nonprofits are there to push policy and solutions. Businesses accelerate solutions.

We all can influence policy. We do it when we vote.

Capital is very efficient.

When a policy is created the capital will flow into it.

Mission based investing.

Cap and trade forces people to innovate.

---

[10]http://ecorner.stanford.edu/authorMaterialInfo.html?mid=1903

Each asset class is being mobilized to solve these problems.

Entrepreneurial Practices for High-Impact Non-Profits

Date: 2008-02-06

Speaker: Christine Benninger (Humane Society)

Link: Entrepreneurial Thought Leaders[11]

The mission carries you through the tough times.

When your back is to the wall is when you become your most creative.

Passion is a double-edged sword.

Passion is very personal. When things are personal people often don't want to compromise.

The less people pay for an animal the more likely they are to turn it in.

The more you pay–people think it is a better product.

---

[11] http://ecorner.stanford.edu/authorMaterialInfo.html?mid=1904

The Path to an Acquisition

Date: 2008-02-13

Speaker: Brett Crosby (Google Analytics)

Link: Entrepreneurial Thought Leaders[12]

Goal wasn't to get every dime out of every customer. Goal was to be the most dominant web analytics product on the market.

Get a good copywriter. Get a good graphics guy.

It is good to have something you're trying to get done.

Go big.

Act big but stay humble.

Try new business models.

Celebrate the crazy moments.

As soon as you understand one job you need to hire someone else to do it and move on.

In your element you can be fast.

Work with what you have.

---

[12]http://ecorner.stanford.edu/authorMaterialInfo.html?mid=1905

Be yourself. Have fun.

Never do dispute resolution over email.

Healthy Entrepreneurship in Medical Devices

Date: 2008-02-20

Speaker: Mir Imran (InCube Laboratories)

Link: Entrepreneurial Thought Leaders[13]

It starts with a problem. The process starts with analysis of the problem and looking at its attributes. How big is the problem? How is it currently solved?

The more time you spend with a problem the better chance you have coming up with a good solution.

When you're looking at unique problems look at European literature. Sometimes they're more open about unique problems.

Evaluate your ideas and kill them because it is much more painful to kill a company or fix a failing company.

Surround yourself with really smart people.

A lot of times companies get into trouble because of people problems.

---

[13] http://ecorner.stanford.edu/authorMaterialInfo.html?mid=1906

You can't find the exact skillset you're looking for. Find somebody who is really good and then modify the plan on the other people you're going to hire.

When you find people that are going to be successful you hang on to them.

You need depth in multiple areas.

In medicine there are a lot of problems that are poorly solved or not solved at all.

Don't fall in love with your ideas. Sometimes the first idea isn't the right idea.

Be a good listener.

Surround yourself with people who are experienced.

Assess what you're getting into upfront.

Market size dictates where you have a product or a company.

Representing the Socially Responsible Enterprise

Date: 2008-02-27

Speaker: Debra Dunn, Jay Coen Gilbert, Bart Houlahan, Andrew Kassoy (B Corporation)

Link: Entrepreneurial Thought Leaders[14]

B Corporations must meet environmental performance standards.

Transparency, accountability, and performance.

The private sector can be a much more powerful engine for social change than the non-profit or government sector can be.

B corporations offers differentiation.

The more you use words the less they mean.

Licensing fee for a B corporation is 10 basis points.

Marketing (or branding) is not an event–it is a process. It is a cumulative process.

The team with the best idea wins.

[14] http://ecorner.stanford.edu/authorMaterialInfo.html?mid=1907

You can't do it alone. It requires a team.

You've got to be a great listener.

Banking on Corporate Culture and Strategy

Date: 2008-03-05

Speaker: Ken Wilcox (Silicon Valley Bank)

Link: Entrepreneurial Thought Leaders[15]

The most important things a company can focus on are its strategy and its culture.

Culture trumps strategy every time.

Desperate people will go to great ends and take great risks.

The world of venture backed companies is global.

Technology companies deposit about seven times what they borrow.

There is no such thing as an underserved niche. Every niche has been discovered. If it is underserved then it likely isn't a good niche.

Culture is the most important part of any organization.

Culture is what motivates.

Hire as diverse a set of people as you possible can.

---

[15] http://ecorner.stanford.edu/authorMaterialInfo.html?mid=1908

People need to work as a team.

Complex and sophisticated problems can only be solved by teams.

Everybody has to have an oar. Everybody has to pull on their oar in unison.

The first source of repayment is cash flow. The second is saleable assets (collateral).

Entrepreneurship That Clicks

Date: 2008-04-09

Speaker: Jeff Housenbold (Shutterfly)

Link: Entrepreneurial Thought Leaders[16]

Entrepreneurship is mostly a state of mind.

Entrepreneurship is about the state of mind of creating new products, of creating new markets, of creating new ideas, and creating new business and capturing some of the economic rents from that vision and the hard work.

Do something that you really love.

There is a pattern in using products and being passionate about them.

You don't know everything. You can't do everything. You're not good at everything.

Understand your strengths and amplify them.

Focus on innovation.

Have a rabbi (someone in the organization who has a propensity for mentorship).

---

[16]http://ecorner.stanford.edu/authorMaterialInfo.html?mid=1971

Do what really interests you.

Go where the money is made in the company.

Solve your boss' and your boss' boss' problems proactively.

Go where there is tremendous growth or complete turnaround.

Don't care about title at the early stages of your career.

Delegate effectively.

Success is not how smart you are but how can you get people to do what you want.

Build great teams.

Find time for the balance in life.

Concentrated Power in a Global Economy

Date: 2008-04-16

Speaker: David Rothkopf (Author)

Link: Entrepreneurial Thought Leaders[17]

Assumption is the world is as it was.

All evidence suggests nation-states are waning in power.

Nations are built to focus within their borders.

Governments don't work. Leave it to the markets.

Markets seek efficiency.

You get efficiency through scale.

Power is concentrated.

20/80 rule is reductive.

All ten of the world's largest defense contractors reside in the U.S.

4,300 religions on the planet.

The middle class has shrunk in every country but India and China.

---

[17] http://ecorner.stanford.edu/authorMaterialInfo.html?mid=1972

The top 10% of the people on the planet control 85% of its wealth.

The top 2% control 40% of the wealth on the plant.

Definition of superclass is people who have influence over the lives of millions of people, across borders, on a regular basis.

Gender and geography are destiny in the global power structure.

Luck is destiny.

All things aren't equal.

The real nature of power is skewed. It is disproportionate.

Globalization is happening. The question is what are you going to do with it? How are you going to make it work?

You have to put in checks and balances.

Rewarding Sky-High Innovation

Date: 2008-04-23

Speaker: Peter Diamandis, George Zachary (X Prize)

Link: Entrepreneurial Thought Leaders[18]

Go back to what you were really passionate about as a kid.

Make a career out of something you really, really passionately love.

If you're going to do something big in this world it is going to be hard.

Life is too short to do things for somebody else.

Insane pressure is the mother of invention.

Opening a frontier, any frontier, is multidisciplinary.

True breakthroughs require taking risks.

If it is a true breakthrough it is a crazy idea.

The average age of the engineers who designed the Apollo program was 26.

The first rule of sales is you have to ask.

---

[18]http://ecorner.stanford.edu/authorMaterialInfo.html?mid=1973

Give people an opportunity to help you.

When you ask for money you get advice. When you ask for advice you get money.

Investing is a transferring of confidence.

Prizes drag regulation in their wake.

There are three phases of a good idea. The first is that people say, "It is crazy and will never work." The next phase is that "it might work but is not worth doing." The third phase is "I told you it was a great idea all along."

Unreeling the Documentary Film

Date: 2008-04-30

Speaker: Anand Chandrasekaran, Michealene C. Risley (Tapestries of Hope)

Link: Entrepreneurial Thought Leaders[19]

Keep your mind open to new possibilities.

Even if you're already doing something it is important to keep an open mind.

Go for broke and fail big.

Tell a powerful story.

Book: Women Who Like the Dark

Don't underestimate the value of Facebook.

It is not very easy to make money on documentaries.

It has to be something you are passionate about.

---

[19] http://ecorner.stanford.edu/authorMaterialInfo.html?mid=1974

The Evolution of Yahoo!

Date: 2008-05-07

Speaker: Sue Decker (Yahoo!)

Link: Entrepreneurial Thought Leaders[20]

Focus on the customer as the guiding light in everything you do.

Top of funnel is creating awareness and brands. As you move down the funnel you create transactions.

Advertisers want to reach whatever consumer is most likely to purchase their product.

Take advantage of scale.

Start with knowing what your customers want.

Stocks are valued looking forward rather than the past.

There is always a price.

The quickest thing you can change is advertising.

Advertising is cyclical with the economy.

If you don't integrate you don't get the power of scale.

People will pay for great, specialized content that is relevant to them.

---

[20]http://ecorner.stanford.edu/authorMaterialInfo.html?mid=1975

The Next Wave of Corporate Philanthropy

Date: 2008-05-14

Speaker: Larry Brilliant (Google.org)

Link: Entrepreneurial Thought Leaders[21]

Ghandi said, "Before you act consider the face of the poorest, most desolate person that you ever have a chance to meet. Remember that person, his life, his circumstance and then ask yourself if that which you are about to do will benefit that person."

The disparity between rich and poor is the greatest today.

Philanthropy has to choose what do we do to make the world better.

We're all in this together.

One world. One health.

People want water, healthcare, and education.

---

[21]http://ecorner.stanford.edu/authorMaterialInfo.html?mid=1976

Music Artists Go Entrepreneurial

Date: 2008-07-24

Speaker: Tony Perkins (AlwaysOn Panel)

Link: Entrepreneurial Thought Leaders[24]

Sometimes you have to take the bitter with the sweet. (Mistah FAB)

Technology has rewritten the business model for the music industry. (MC Hammer)

Everybody is an artist. Everybody is a blogger. (Chamillionaire)

The Internet offers artists free distribution and free marketing. (QJ3)

The world is at your fingertips. (Chamillionaire)

People want to associate with a winner. (MC Hammer)

You can't give away everything. (MC Hammer)

You've got to humble yourself down. (Chamillionaire)

What is a handshake to you is to somebody a lifetime memory. (Mistah FAB)

---

[24]http://ecorner.stanford.edu/authorMaterialInfo.html?mid=2047

A VC Perspective on the Life Sciences

Date: 2008-05-28

Speaker: Beth Seidenberg (KPCB)

Link: Entrepreneurial Thought Leaders[23]

The most important thing is leadership.

They look for companies serving large markets.

A sense of urgency is critical.

Being first matters. Being the best matters.

Intellectual property protection is important for life sciences and cleantech.

Know how to put financing together or know somebody who can help you.

Every company goes to the ICU at least once.

You have to be nimble to deal with crises.

Sometimes you need to be a psychologist and a therapist (when bringing great people into a company).

You don't need to start out with business expertise. Find somebody who does.

---

[23] http://ecorner.stanford.edu/authorMaterialInfo.html?mid=1978

Under the Microscope: Socially Responsible Biotech

Date: 2008-05-21

Speaker: John Melo (Amyris Biotechnologies)

Link: Entrepreneurial Thought Leaders[22]

Don't think about the technology. Think about what the world needs.

Pick a scaleable project that is low cost.

Get as much efficiency into your process as possible.

A resource rich environment doesn't necessarily get the most innovation.

Being able to adapt helps you learn in environments where you have no answers.

Being smart isn't an advantage. Be able to do something with those smarts in a team environment.

You can attract people by having an exciting project to work on.

---

[22]http://ecorner.stanford.edu/authorMaterialInfo.html?mid=1977

Interesting opportunities always present themselves. Be patient.

Don't stop pursuing your dream.

Analytics is the end game. (MC Hammer)

Analytics let you put your promoting dollars in the right places. (MC Hammer)

You have to interact with the fans. (Mistah FAB)

If some people know how smart you are they aren't going to talk in front of you. (Chamillionaire)

Innovation is what makes you stand out from other people. (Chamillionaire)

Don't talk about it. Just show people. (Chamillionaire)

Even a genius asks questions. (Mistah FAB)

If you're smart enough to know something you're smart enough to know you know not much at all and there is always more to learn. (Mistah FAB)

The strive for, the thirst for, knowledge is always a beautiful quest. (Mistah FAB)

Thanks for Reading

Thank you for reading *Execution and Other Lessons*. If you enjoyed it you can visit the PersonalOpz blog[25] to read other tips I've accumulated on business and life. There you can also sign up for the mailing list where you'll be sent future books for free.

Please don't hesitate to email me (will@personalopz.com) with any questions or comments.

Thanks again,

Will

---

[25] http://www.personalopz.com/blog/

www.ingramcontent.com/pod-product-compliance
Lightning Source LLC
Chambersburg PA
CBHW071823170526
45167CB00003B/1396